FORCES OF IMAGINATION

FORCES OF IMAGINATION

Writing on Writing

Barbara Guest

KELSEY ST. PRESS

Kelsey St. Press wishes to express appreciation to Hadley Haden-Guest.

Library of Congress Cataloging-in-Publication Data
Guest, Barbara.
  Forces of imagination : writing on writing / Barbara Guest.
     p. cm.
   ISBN 0-932716-64-4 (alk. paper) — ISBN 0-932716-61-X (pbk. : alk.
paper)
 1. Poetry—Authorship. 2. Poetics. I. Title.
   PS3513.U44F67 2003
   808.1—dc21

                              2002155028

Cover and interior images by Laurie Reid (see colophon).

Kelsey St. Press
50 Northgate Avenue
Berkeley, California 94708
510 845-2260
kelseyst.com

Distributed by
Small Press Distribution
510 524-1668 or 800 869-7553
spdbooks.org

NATIONAL
ENDOWMENT
FOR THE ARTS

Publication of this book was made possible
in part by grants from the California Arts Council
and the National Endowment for the Arts.

Contents

▼

▼

EDITORS' NOTE

This collection by Barbara Guest has been drawn from talks, published and unpublished essays, poems and short pieces—writings that span a number of decades. Recurring key ideas, quoted phrases, observations concerning poets, painters, cities and architectural sites important to Guest's vision reappear in varying contexts. We have let repetitions stand as insight into Guest's work as a poet, novelist, biographer, and art critic throughout a productive and illustrious career.

Kelsey St. Press

Known truths, however, may take a different appearance, and be conveyed to the mind by a new train of intermediate images . . .

. . . to invest abstract ideas with form, and animate them with activity, has always been the right of poetry . . .

. . . a palace must have passages; a poem must have transitions.

—Samuel Johnson

———————

Dr. Johnson compiled the first dictionary for the eighteenth century;
he was one of the great minds of his time, also known for his association
with James Boswell, who wrote the Life of Johnson.

Radical Poetics and Conservative Poetry

Everything we loved, emulated was attached to the lyric modernism of Baudelaire and Mallarmé's later writing. Walter Benjamin wrote in the late 1930s that *Les Fleurs du Mal* was the last lyric work that had a European repercussion.

In the not too far off future the curtain will be drawn on Modernism as it enters history. Already the shades are listing as Modernism begins to cross the border, exulting in a new freedom called the past. The forms of poetry, too, are restlessly releasing themselves. Having feasted on Modernism they are readying for a new patrol into less inhibited—and what is glimpsed as a more fractured—territory.

Meanwhile the battle lines are still drawn between radical and conservative poetry, as if no one had discovered that long ago Mallarmé had solved that issue. It is said that conservative poetry is the only guide from which one can look backward, rather than forward. Its strength lies in repetition as a long line of flow assembles between the lampposts of the past, the landscapes of the past and the neighborliness of what are called "loved" objects.

Because of its ability to recognize a subject not for its substantive value, but for its definition, conservative poetry takes issue with reality as it assembles itself in a poem. For instance a planted tree is seen as planted with roots in the ground, perhaps a nearby trowel and a parent or child further off to the left watching the clearly delineated leaves, and the moral is an esteemed one placing value on the absoluteness of growing things.

The radical tree might be made of bones and the only clue to its recognition is that the poet has called it a bone-tree. And yet this tree is about growth and these are the eminent qualities of bones. But the radical poet draws no moral from the assemblage. The moral is in the hands of the reader.

In conservative poetry the poets live in a complementary world, without being aware of what surrounds them. They exist in a space hemmed in by other trees that are called "real trees." This poetry offers the promise of reality, yet in a defined space the poem, itself, is never free.

The radical poem suffers from a few of the same difficulties, but in the defenestrating process of saying something new the structure of the poem suffers and the poet becomes engaged in a search for supports that will hold together the poem; and these supports are so new themselves, like spandex, they must be marketed to realize their future. And this uses up invaluable creative time.

Meanwhile the conservative poet is comfortably ensconced in the tried leather of a poem and the voice whether from Odessa or London or Cairo is welcome, because although the sensibility may be tired the words when they arrive are refreshingly old and they look like cherries or lilies and can be understood. The poem projects meanings or values; it creates an atmosphere of security and that is like velvet.

I don't believe we need worry about the conservative poem with its borrowed ancestry. Although the heritage of the radical poem is even longer, I want to reassure myself about its immediate contests.

A diversion was created when Art was given the vulgar guise of Postmodernism. This art had nothing to do with Modernism, of course. An invented term betrays the ethos of the society that accepts it. And perhaps there are practitioners who might be called Postmodern in their vandalism. But in order to accept this term we have to believe that Modernism, itself, is finished. Like throwing a bathing cap into the divine flux.

The conservative artist would like nothing better than to believe in the demise of Modernism. It is a subject that haunts this artist continually. The life of the conservative artist is preoccupied with avoiding the hurdles of Modernism.

The radical issues of a poem are infinite and this accounts for the immodesty of the poet who confronts endless space. This imposed immodesty needs to be protected in the closed environment in which an artist lives, subject to regulation and mandated law. The modesty of the conservatives is confined to the background of their work. In the forefront, in public, they are vociferous, as if they read with many tongues. Actually they are engaged in temporary struggles, with the use of the sledgehammer against ice.

Lest I be accused of warfare with metaphors I would like to include a personal comment on the reception of Vaçlav Havel in the United States

Senate, where he was welcomed with open arms as if he possessed the magic to release its practitioners from mendacity, as if Cicero once more had appeared to castigate the rogue Catiline. "O tempora O mores!"

It is a subject for fiction, even hallucination, to suppose that an American artist would have been permitted to impose such radical opinions on the American Senate. And yet Havel was uproariously welcomed and real tears were shed.

Imagination

In the introduction to a new edition of *My Sister — Life,* we learn that Pasternak was once asked: "What is Art?" When asked the same question, Verlaine had answered that it was music. Pasternak thought art was greater than music, "for it was concerned with greatness itself." Finally the poet decided that Art was "grandeur." We can see the poet at Peredelkino, his retreat in the last days of his own grandeur, considering a question put to him more than once, a tired question, for which he must have been prepared. But no, he decided to speak again and he said to his questioners and friends that "ultimately art derives from human dignity, from charity." Then he became more enthusiastic. Having uttered the expected words, he turned to his interlocutor once again, and we have the feeling that history is now going to enter: "One must live in sovereign freedom like a king, never surrendering to temporal authority or traditions however deeply rooted, but out of one's own acquired perfections, honest with himself." That is, one must live out of oneself.

I want to speak about living out of oneself, as this will bring us to the inner kingdom of the imagination.

Imagination has its orderly zones. It is not always the great tumultuous sea on which we view a small boat. It can lie behind hedges, hide in boxes, even suffer the touch of exile in a world subsisting on invention.

Classical imagination contributes to the beauty of form out of which it grows and which Homer brings to us as he imagines the beauty of Helen or Achilles, the sinew of the arms of oarsmen. Out of myth arose this stupendous imagination and its direct inheritor was the sculpture of Phidias, who molded with his imagination, not from real life only—and here I want to insist that there is no conflict between realism and imagination. The Charioteer is clearly representational and clearly imaginary. The classic form is abstract and concrete at the same time.

In Neoclassicism, to reiterate for my purposes ideas with which you are already familiar, poets borrowed from their reading to subsidize, to endorse their imaginations, which otherwise would have deteriorated into domesticity—given the enclosed world they were now in—as opposed to the seas of Classicism. They turned to libraries to embellish themselves with the ideas of others, just as in early Medievalism clerics had copied from the texts of ancients, and speech and learning were handed down to us.

I bring up this distinction between Classicism and Neoclassicism, because I believe the poetics of today has progressed from Classicism to Neoclassicism and this is an honest removal although we may regret it.

In appropriation of texts, in subsistence on the words of others, even from the contemporary world, imagination must have its proper position, because only imagination can return the texts to life. One of the implicit properties of imagination is that it resists clear and absolute meaning. If unrestricted, we are welcomed into an activity that guides us into the realm of the self, the oneself where creativity breathes.

There is no substitute for imagination. Words deprived of their stability —that is if not fed by the imagination—rush around attempting to attach themselves to a surface. They have no stabilized vocation; they become furtive, ready to sell themselves. Wordsworth, not immune to appropriating landscape, wrote:

> Language, if it do not uphold, and feed, and leave in quiet, like the power of gravitation or the air we breathe, is a counter-spirit, unremittingly and noiselessly at work to derange, to subvert, to lay waste, to vitiate, and to dissolve.

It is the counter-spirit we must beware of, even in the presence of despairing academic anxiety that—overwhelmed by the creative spirit, angered by imagination that disrupts its formulaic view of life—would like to convert imagination into a conservative toy.

In such an atmosphere of controlled tedium it is always refreshing to turn to a poet such as Jules Laforgue, who in 1883 wrote:

> In the flashes of identity between subject and object lie the nature of genius. And any attempt to codify such flashes is but an academic pastime.

From these "flashes of identity"—marvelous phrase—and above academic anxiety rises an elite structure, elite not because it is marble, but because it is rock in which Art survives in every era sustained by desire and necessity.

Finally, in case we become discouraged or overwhelmed or even disappointed in our era, in the state of our art, I would like to remind us of the remark Valéry made in 1933, a year that was to initiate the close of an era: "Profound changes are impending in the ancient craft of the Beautiful."

————————

Presented at the Poetry Project, St. Mark's Church-in-the-Bowery, New York City, as part of an evening of four lectures on "Poetry 1990: The State of the Art" on May 5, 1990.

Invisible Architecture

There is an invisible architecture often supporting
  the surface of the poem, interrupting the progress of the poem. It
reaches
into the poem
in search of
  an identity with the poem;

its object is to possess the poem for a brief time, even as an apparition
appears. An invisible architecture upholds the poem while allowing a
moment of relaxation for the unconscious. A period of emotional sug-
gestion, of lapse, of reliance on the conscious substitute words pushed
toward the bridge of the architecture. An architecture in the period before
the poem finds an exact form and vocabulary—,

before the visible appearance of the poem on the page and the invisible
approach to its composition. Reaching out to develop the poem there are
interruptions, some apparently for no reason—something else is happening, the poet has no control—the poem begins to quiver, to hesitate,
to become insubstantial, the desire of poetry to elevate itself, to become
stronger. . . . The poem is fragile. It needs to reach through the armed
vehicle of the poem,
      to loosen the armed hand

Losing the arrogance of dominion over the poem to an invisible hand, the poet campaigns for a passage over which the poet has control. Yet the unstableness of the poem is important.

Also the frequent lapses of control of the poem.
The writer only slowly retains power over the poem, physical power, when the poem breaks away from authority of the invisible architecture.

This invisible authority may be the unconscious that dwells on the lower level, in a substratum beneath the surface of the poem and possesses its own reference. A fluidity only enters the poem when it becomes more openly aware of itself.

By whom or by what agency is the behavior of the poem suggested, by what invisible architecture, we ask, is the poem developed? The Surrealists taught us to wander freely on the page, releasing mechanical birds, if we so desire, to nest in the invisible handwriting of composition. There is always something within poetry that desires the invisible.

The desire of the poet to control. This control was earlier destructive to the interior of the poem, to its infrastructure. There is something deliberate about this practice of control by consciousness. It includes the question that is undefined, the behavior of the poem. By whom or by what agency is this decided, by what invisible architecture is the poem developed?

Appeared in INPRINT, *November 2002; Dorothy Terry and Maureen Michaels, editors.*

A Reason for Poetics

For all his purple, the purple bird must have
Notes for his comfort that he may repeat
Through the gross tedium of being rare.

— Wallace Stevens

The Infancy of Poetics

The poem begins in silence.

Poetic Codes

A pull in both directions between the physical reality of place and the metaphysics of space. This pull will build up a tension within the poem giving a view of the poem from both the interior and the exterior.

Ideally a poem will be both mysterious (incunabula, driftwood of the unconscious), and organic (secular) at the same time. If the tension becomes irregular, like a heartbeat, then a series of questions enters the poem. What is now happening? What does the poem, itself, consider to be its probabilities? The poem needs to take care not to flounder, or become rigid, or to come to such a halt the reader hangs over a sudden cliff. It is noticeable that a poem has a secret grip of its own, separate from its creator.

The poem is quite willing to forget its begetter and take off in its own direction. It likes to be known as spontaneous. Some poets then become firm and send out admonitory hints. Others become anxious. A few become pleased with the trickster and want to adopt it. There are moments when mistaken imageries can lead in interesting directions. Poets even try to charm the poem. We have all taken these positions.

The conflict between a poet and the poem creates an atmosphere of mystery. When this mystery is penetrated, when the dark reaches of the poem succumb and shine with a clarity projected by the mental lamp of the reader, then an experience called *illumination* takes place. This is the most beautiful experience literature can present us with, and more precious for being extremely rare, arrived at through concentration, through meditation of the poem, through those faculties we often associate with a religious experience, as indeed it is. The reader is converted to the poem. (Invisible magic also passes between poet and reader.)

Mystery, with its element of surprise and, better word, audacity. At once unexpected dramas have entered the poem. The search for its originating mystery now becomes an adventure. Poet and reader perform together on a highwire strung on a platform between their separated selves. Now an applause for the shared vigilance.

The usefulness of the tension set up in a poem is to arrange its dimensions. The poem stretches, looking outwardly and inwardly, thus obtaining a plasticity that the flat, the basic words—what we call the language of a poem—demands and, further, depends upon. This cannot be achieved through language alone, but arrives from tensions placed on the poem's structure: variability of meter, fleeting moods of expression, trebled sound.

Each poet owns a private language. The poet relies on the pitch within the ear. The ear is also a private affair, and so is pitch. Much poetry betrays a tin ear. There is also trouble in possessing perfect pitch, which can lead to an obsessive need to listen to it. Like ravens quothing. But this is not a common trouble. Pitch and ear are the servants of language and cannot make their living anywhere else, even by escapades. Language can lead to trouble when words are selected solely for their sound, and meaning is then forced to hurry along after, trying to catch up. Sometimes it is necessary to dispense with a word, or rather to be cautious, when it intrudes upon form.

The structure of the poem should create an embrasure inside of which language is seated in watchful docility, like the unicorn. Poems develop a terrible possessiveness toward their language because they admire the decoration of their structure.

The Poetics of Survival

Poetry sometimes develops a grayness; the light can never get in. The surface is smudgy. Cézanne was irritated by this murkiness in painting and complained "the contour eludes me."

How splendid when a poem is both prospective and introspective, obeying tensions within itself until a classic plasticity is reached.

I have little regard for poems of mine which have become votives of obsolete reactions. These poems appear to have no conscience, and worse, are passionless.

There is nothing fearsome about the chrome attic. There are more mad poets out on the lawn. And very few wear cloud trousers.

I wish the Emperor's new clothes were less a visual phenomenon and more poetry's plaintive sigh.

And then there is saving laughter. I don't mean by "laughter" what is known as "comic relief." That seems to me to be part of a philosophical argument surrounding questions such as "why did Shakespeare, or Meredith bring in such and such a character?" My laughter is bittersweet and brings us closer to irony, the mole of poetry. Irony is a coagulant of pain when the subject of the poem (the interior meaning) begins to draw blood. Robust poets, it seems to me, too seldom acknowledge this weapon against poetry's sores, the most suppurating of which is sentimentality.

Mandelstam once wrote of "sound spilling into fingers." That could be the noise of a poem when it experiences an ecstasy of recognition.

To keep the poem alive after its many varnishings.

———————

Appeared in Ironwood, *No. 24, 1984; Michael Cuddihy, editor.*

The Element of Surprise

The Element of surprise in a poem,

in its development, in the handle it seizes to bring itself upright, on tiptoe.

Finally to survey the domain of a poem. Or to hide in the confines of the
poem until the line is ready to reveal itself.   Counting ten   waiting

for emotion to gather in its throat,
    to hoist itself into the center of the domain of the poem.

Following sensibility, timorous even, but sure of the location where the
poem shall reveal itself.   A sense of timing.
    As Picasso remarked,
        "It's always something else in the end."

                            to reach that surprise.

Poetry the True Fiction

The title I originally gave to this talk is "How I got out of Poetry into Prose." This title came to me so quickly because at that time I was encouraging myself to write fiction, and I thought I would discuss the dimensions of fiction with you. However, I was disturbed by this title and rightly so; had I been more intuitive of my own perceptions, and had I listened to the poet William Cowper, who wrote "Poets are seldom good for anything except in rime," I would have entitled this talk more sensitively: "Poetry the True Fiction."

Why has the word fiction become associated with prose? It is poetry that transforms the real world into fiction. Mallarmé understood this. He wrote: "The true fiction is that of the poet."

Mallarmé regarded poetry as an art dedicated to fictionalization, an *"art consacré aux fictions"* where the concrete object is "bathed in a new atmosphere," lifted out of itself to become a fiction. The poet is not there only to share a poetic communication, but to stimulate an imaginative speculation on the nature of reality.

Do you recall the poem of Wallace Stevens "Notes Towards a Supreme Fiction"? And have you considered what the title meant, or what was the underlying meaning of the title? I'm at the point where I take everything he says for granted—the moon being made of ice-cream, etc.—so I never questioned his meaning until the other day when I was considering poetry as fiction. In his published correspondence I found a letter from Stevens to his publisher, the Cummington Press. He wrote:

> The title of the book will be *Notes Toward a Supreme Fiction.* Each of the three groups will develop or at least have some relation to a particular note: as
>
> I
> It must be abstract
>
> II
> It must change
>
> III
> It must give pleasure.
>
> These are three notes by way of defining the characteristics of supreme fiction. By supreme fiction, of course, I mean poetry.

The fiction of the poet is part of restless twentieth century perception based on the discovery that reality is a variable, and is open-ended in form and matter.

And now that we recognize poetry activates an established world of fiction, I should like to discuss the supremacies or the necessaries of poetry that enable it to transform reality. I would like to speak about Vision and Imagination.

Vision is part of the poet's spiritual life of which the poem, itself, is a résumé. The "spirit" or the "vision" of a poem arises from the contents of the poet's unconscious. Let us say the vision of a poem has above it that "halo" you see in religious paintings when an act of special beneficence is being enacted by one of the persons within the picture and that person is given a halo. The poem is our act of special beneficence and the poet is rewarded this halo. The poet is unaware of the halo, just as in the paintings the persons are unaware of the halo, but it is there as a reward for a particular unconscious state of immanence. Now I am not speaking of a religious state of grace in regard to the poem, the poem let us say is its own religion. I am using the word "halo" because you and I can see it in the painting, and this halo has a value to us; it reflects a state of mind, or a condition that the mind has attained.

The halo has detected the magnetic field into which the energy of the poem is being directed.

I would like you to understand that I am using the words "spirit," "vision," "halo" because I wish to lift us upward away from the desk of a projected poem. I want to emphasize that the poem needs to have a spiritual or metaphysical life if it is going to engage itself with reality.

As closely as possible in the world I am representing here the poet wishes to align the contents of the poem with the vision which directs it. When this occurs we say of the poem that it has "wings."

It is possible that words may occur in a fixed space and sequence so that they are called "words of a poem." We say the poem is made of words. And it is true that many poems are constructed solely of words. These are the words that sit on paper without vision. We all have read these poems and we know that after we have read them we feel curiously bereft. Our expectations of ennoblement by the poem have been disappointed by the lackluster condition of the poem.

We decide that this poem is not very inspired. And what do we mean by this? We desired "inspiration," that the poem contain within it evidences of the spirit of poetry.

We have learned that words are only utensils. They are inorganic unless there is a spirit within the poem to elevate it, to give it "wings," so that the poem may soar above the page and enter our consciousness where we may if we wish give it a long life, a longer life than would occur when the poem lies without elevation on a piece of paper.

There is no reason to signal any decade or era as deficient of vision. Words on a page are deficient of vision and this may occur in any epoch. We are particularly nervous about our own era because we are at the turn of a century which is most usually designated a time of decadence. We see this everywhere, unfortunately in the decay of institutions, but mostly there is a demise of the spirit and that is what should concern us, because poetry will reflect this spiritual absence.

Words without vision are deprived of stability. They cling desperately to a mirrored surface in an effort to attach themselves to a surface, because they have no direction and no stabilized vocation. They become furtive, these words, thirsty for a version of themselves that contains no failure of vision. Words contain their own beauty of face, but they desire an occupation. They cannot exist on beauty or necessity alone.

Words of the poem need dimension. They desire finally—an education in space. The poet needs to understand the auditory and spatial needs of a poem to free it so that the poem can locate its own movement, so that it is freed to find its own voice, its own rhythm or accent or power.

Wordsworth wrote: *Language if it do not uphold, and feed, and leave in quiet like the power of gravitation or air we breathe, is a counter-spirit, unremittingly and noiselessly at work to derange, to subvert, to lay waste, to vitiate, and to dissolve.*

It is not the flash of brilliance appropriated in a technique that quenches the pathos of a deprived poem. Although we must not neglect those qualities Leopardi admired in Horace: "courageous metaphors, singular and far-fetched epithets, inversions, placement of words, suppressions" —recognize them? They appear in our own shifting techniques.

Regard the poem as plastic. It is moveable, touchable. It is a viable breathing substance. Nothing is more useless than a poem with a dull sheen that refuses to move, that is inert. This is the essence of dullness and our eyes run quickly past it.

A poem has not only a voice, but a mouth and the mouth must move just as much as the voice must speak and it must not be careless in its speech. And flesh of a poem. Even as a painting has flesh. The vibrancy of its skin.

The artist de Kooning wrote that in the Renaissance drawing started to tremble because it wanted to go places. He also added that what we call subject matter was then painting itself. There was no subject matter.

De Kooning also observed that at this time the artist was too perplexed to be sure of himself. Later subject matter ruled the arts. And, said de Kooning, when you think of all the life and death problems in the art of the Renaissance, who cares if a Chevalier is laughing or that a young girl has a red blouse on. De Kooning is telling us to beware of description or "subject matter." In other words to think of the poem itself.

Vision and plasticity are the two essentials of a poem. The spirit of the poem and its moveable form, not its "adjustable" form. Then we get into posing or Chevaliers or red blouses.

I hope you realize that in all these words I have gathered together, or if you wish in the few words I have gathered, I have not come directly to Imagination.

I have first wanted to prepare the ground for Imagination. For us to consider the spirit of the poem, its physicality and its spatial intensity. Now I would like to speak about Imagination because it is really my favorite topic. Without Imagination the red blouse is a piece of description, without Imagination the poem is only words on a page.

This is a very large subject Imagination. I shall touch upon it only briefly. But I must speak about it, because for me it is the single most important element of poetry and it is my touchstone. When I examine a poem it is not for its form or style or even gravity but I look for its imaginative powers. I find that Imagination comes before style or technique. How empty all the dazzle of style is without the immediacy of the touch of Imagination. And Imagination the changeling can sting you with its fictive barbs.

Coleridge wrote *Biographia Literaria* in his youth when he was trembling with imaginative power. The book is essential, I believe, for the distinction he makes between Imagination and Fancy. Fancy is delightful, evocative, alas charming, but with fancy you leave those words on the page. A good many poets are endowed with a lively fancy, many more than those who live in the Imagination. Fancy is useful and can shake people up and present itself century after century as the new. But it is not art; it is games.

Imagination lives with the visionary. When you touch its glass there is a ring. The French have a phrase *"clair-obscur"* which translates as obscure light and means the mysterious side of thought. That could well define Imagination.

We tend to think of it as so lively it pierces walls, but that liveliness is fancy. Imagination is *clair-obscur.* It is also "the absent flower" of Mallarmé. A turbulent presence. And we must acknowledge this "turbulent presence" because it is there to save the poem from a disobedient disregard of its own nature.

There will always be poetry, in its search for a language, a desire for the liberation of the Imagination.

André Breton said, "to imagine is to see."

───────

Read at the State University of New York at Buffalo, April, 1992. Published in Carcanet, 1995; Michael Schmidt, editor. Also published in the Exact Change Yearbook, 1995; Peter Gizzi, editor.

Why They Are Called Tales

Tales are stories about stories; they are brought to us from memory and arrive with often an antique finish; they are also arrived from the deep unconscious of a country or place. Tales may be a residue from childhood. They live in a more dimensional world than a story that is a reportage, or a story that is about something, or that is current in the world of reporting. I believe that a Tale has more magic than a story. It breathes within a separate world of memory or desire. Its remoteness from the center of things is what is endearing about a Tale and it doesn't tell the truth about itself; it tells us what it dreams about. And remember that a Tale arises from the imagination, and this is what makes a Tale live in another dimension.

So from this other dimension we advance the Tale into our dimension, which means the Tale has been on a long trip when it arrives on the page; this means the Tale can be called more dimensional than a story. Which is not to denigrate the story but to say that the Tale has a twist attached to it; so it is a twisted story with a real tail.

I thought at first I would write a worldly real story and I did, but it was too long. I wanted to make it skinny, but the adjectives and adverbs and the daily tasks of living made my story too big, like a swelling. So I began the process of thinning down the story. I really wanted "and," "but," "the" to disappear so I took them out — still, things were dangling. And I bumped into those things. Then I wrote a little story, but it was boring. Then I added a paragraph to it, but all you could see was that it was dressed in a paragraph. I put a name to each story, quite properly, and put this title at the top of the page, but the story looked top heavy. So I took the title away and I liked it better, but I was told that stories had titles so put it back in. No one will know what you are writing about unless you give a story a title, I was told.

At this point I decided I didn't want to write a "story." But my fingers were empty and I missed my stories that were told in a manner I didn't like. It was then I discovered that the word "story" was misleading and if I substituted "tale" I could do anything I liked. So I wrote "Tales" without any fixings and called them *Stripped Tales*.

———

Stripped Tales *by Barbara Guest was published by Kelsey St. Press in 1995.*

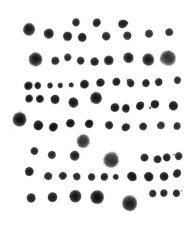

Shifting Persona

I

The windows are normally independent of one another, although you may pass back and forth from one view to the other. This absurd inter-dependence is like a lark at break of day. The altitude is assumed by the upper window. The lark song. The other window is the lark.

The person inside a literary creation can be both viewer and insider. The window is open and the bird flies in. It closes and a drama between the bird and its environment begins.

When the person who is you is the viewer, you believe an extraordinary strength exists in that position. You are outside the arena of dispute or creativity or blasphemy, dwelling in a private space where emotive spec-ulation is stronger than fact or action, each of which passes before you in an attempt at dissimulation which you are free to dispute. This is called the orchid position, because of the extravagant attention the viewer demands.

Sometimes it is the flap of a tent held back, or a cushion pushed next to a door, or a turban lifted over one eye—even a mountain top is offered where the person who is outside the scene can take up an observation post and gaze closely down into the valley.

Without the person outside there would be no life inside. The scene relies on that exterior person to explain the plangent obsessions with which art is adorned.

Yet inside the window is the person who is you, who are now looking out, shifted from the observer to the inside person and this shows in your work. When you are the inside person you can be both heavy and delicate, depending upon your mood; you have a sense of responsibility totally different from the you outside. You occupy the lotus position.

You are depending upon yourself to a degree that can cause extreme unease, but this is acute to all species of creativity. You find you cannot always depend upon yourself as absorbedly as when you assumed the orchid positions because you are more vulnerable, dependent upon the psychic phenomena that occupy your meditation. The lotus position is one of exaggerated self-dependency, in which the eye goes inward so frequently that rest stops are required, something like paragraphic encasings.

These rest stops can be seen in the shifts that take place between the persona of the creator and the persona of the observer. In a well-developed persona the shifts take place before our eyes without revealing themselves, as if gauze had been spun especially for the purpose; and a curtain falls slyly between the persona of the person and the persona that is now accepted. We travel back to the mountaintop and the valley with the shifting of spatial contacts.

II

The ability to project both windows is a sign of originality and is rare. In writing concealed within a limited physical environment, as in the work of Jane Austen, the threat of claustrophobia hangs over the whole body of the novels. In order to relieve this environmental tension, the writer with her strokes of genius elevates the characters above a physical dimension, so that although their persons appear to inhabit a closed drawing-room they are actually removed from the interior to the exterior as they move beyond their limited space through the projection of the author.

They are persons who are capable in their minds, even in an obtuse mind, of looking outside themselves into another place, of shifting their persons. They are relieved of ordained claustrophobia, as is the reader, who might be stuck in that drawing room, who is lifted by the author's inked quill, her euphemism for time, to project beyond singularity.

She has even trained us to watch for the apparitions of ourselves moving alongside the characters. This is on a grand scale, her knowledge of sequence in time caught in a limited physical dimension. The person of the author travels from afar.

III

There is a book about Picasso that records him during his labors while attempting to create his version of *Las Meninas* of Velázquez. What emerges from this devastating account is his conflict with the person of Velázquez as Picasso attempted to stabilize his own persona. Picasso consistently refused to consider his position as revisionist.

Picasso went into the Velázquez painting very far. Yet his enormous struggle, which involved his wife and friends, took place far less within the realm of art than in the psychological struggle of an artist to survive the atmosphere of an originating persona. We are also aware of Picasso's need to endow Velázquez with the Picasso persona.

The painting of Velázquez is even more complicated as several persons compete for the dominating person within *Las Meninas*.

> Picasso said it was a very peculiar affair. Velázquez had painted the King and Queen in the mirror as if they were outside the canvas—which is the fact—but as if it was they who were painting the canvas, since he, Velázquez was inside it with Las Meninas.

> And we said it was an even more peculiar affair for Picasso to paint in that position, while Picasso painted the mirror in which he might have added himself to the King and Queen, who in fact must be on the same side as Velázquez opposite Las Meninas, etc. etc.[1]

Finally out of the hundreds of studies Picasso made of this painting, one in particular succeeds. It is called "The Studio" and there are no persons inside that space.

One of the lessons to be learned from this wildly shortened account of Picasso and *Las Meninas* is that the deliberate ambiguity of the reigning person produces the Velázquez painting's magnificent climaxes, and prevents revision of the work of the originating person. *Las Meninas* has added to the mystery of the person in art.

IV

In *The Uses of Literature,* Italo Calvino writes (I quote from him because he has so rapidly summed up the stunning performance of Flaubert):

> Gustave Flaubert the author of the complete works of Gustave Flaubert projects outside himself the Gustave Flaubert who is the author of Madame Bovary, who in turn projects from himself the character of a middle-class married woman in Rouen, Emma Bovary, who projects from herself that Emma Bovary whom she dreams of being. . . . It was Flaubert himself who gave us the precise clue to this with his famous phrase, "Mme. Bovary, c'est moi."[2]

V

The person with the omnipotence of a cloud hovers over a poem pointing to the direction that it should take.

The poem's concealed autobiography. A memoir of itself which is released as it becomes a presence existing in time.

When the poem is on its feet, to leave it alone to express its own person. The relief from the intensity of the poem's presence as it heats up.

An astonishment throughout the poem at the vibrations of its ego. "I" becomes the bystander and the poem is propelled by the force of the "person" stripped bare.

Richard Wollheim writes: "The artist is essentially a spectator of his work."[3]

VI

A landscape appears before us, solitary in its incidents of meadow broken by low running water, the sky dour, the earth in twists moving like the water into continuous dark drainage. This landscape appears solitary and yet there in the short grass is the hidden person placed there by the writer who desired a human instrument to bear witness to this attempt to construct with a fictional or real landscape a syllabus of art.

The person is given a place of habitation within the construction and endowed with a knowledge not only of the force of nature, but the aesthetic purpose behind the writer's decision to create this scene.

This witness, positioned inside the work of art, conveys to us the secret intent of the writer so that following the instructions now transmitted we may work our way through to the pitch of the art before us, the center where the writing rocks back and forth before taking its plunge into space.

The person is our conduit. Hidden arms are stretched pointing to the variations, the hollows, the deliberate judgments of time within the work of art.

The person has a voice. It echoes the tone of the writer and it is this echoing voice that assembles what we call the "tone" of poetry or prose.

It is the gathering together of varying instructions by the concealed person that presents us with what we may call a "reliable" landscape.

First appeared in the Poetics Journal, *no. 9, 1990; Lyn Hejinian and Barrett Watten, editors. Reprinted in* The American Poetry Review, *September/October, 2002; Arthur Vogelsang, editor.*

1 *Helene Parmelini.* Picasso Plain *(New York: St. Martin's Press, 1963).*

2 *Italo Calvino,* The Uses of Literature, *translated by Patrick Creagh (San Diego: Harcourt, Brace, Jovanovich, 1982).*

3 *Richard Wollheim.* Painting as an Art. The A.W. Mellon Lectures in the Fine Arts *(Princeton: Princeton University Press, 1984).*

Survival

The rare, the beautiful, the spatial Mondrian

of 1922. *Composition with*

Blue, Black, Yellow, and Red—how direct the title is. Was reproduced in

the Art Section of the *New York Times* on January 7, 2000. We are grateful to the Harvard Museum, which has acquired this masterpiece so pris-
tine and fresh, sheltered in a private collection in Holland. The painting
has never left Holland, even for a journey to be on display, never cleaned,
restored or damaged, and even retains its original wood strip frame. The
spirit of Mondrian, bruised in other paintings, somehow meddled with,
survives in this painting.

Intact even in photography. "Shiny black lines, fine brushwork
subtle grey tones, and sharp primary colors," we see how Mondrian "carefully adjusted the lines and planes as they reached the edge of the canvas."

As they touch the edge of Modernity.

On the value of criticism from painters, rather than writers

"Even when crippled by arthritis, Titian
    kept on painting Virgins in that luminous light,
    as if he'd just heard about them."

"Those old guys had everything in place,
    the Virgin and God and technique, but they
    kept it up like they were still looking for
    something. It's very mysterious."

"You have to keep on the edge of something,
    all the time, or the picture dies."

—Willem de Kooning

The Blue Stairs

There is no fear
in taking the first step
or the second
or the third

                                        having a position
                                        between several Popes

In fact the top
can be reached
without disaster

                                        precocious

The code
consists in noticing
the particular shade
of the staircase

                                        occasionally giving way
                                        to the emotions

It has been chosen
discriminately

To graduate
the dimensions
ease them into sight

                      republic of space

Radiant deepness
a thumb
passed over it

                      disarming
                      as one who executes robbers

Waving the gnats
and the small giants
aside

                      balancing

How to surprise
a community
by excellence

somehow it occurred

                                                  living a public life

The original design
was completed
no one complained

In a few years
it was forgotten

                                        floating

It was framed
like any other work of art
not too ignobly

                                        kicking the ladder away

Now I shall tell you
why it is beautiful

Design: extraordinary
color: cobalt blue

                                        secret platforms

Heels twist it
into shape

It has a fantastic area
made for a tread
that will ascend

Being humble
i.e. productive

Its purpose
is to take you upward

On an elevator
of human fingerprints
of the most delicate
fixity

Being practical
and knowing its denominator

To push
one foot ahead of the other

Being a composite
which sneers at marble

                                        all orthodox movements

It has discovered
in the creak of a footstep
the humility of sound

Spatially selective
using this counterfeit
of height

To substantiate
a method of progress

Reading stairs
as interpolation
in the problem of gradualness

        with a heavy and pure logic

The master builder
acknowledges this

As do the artists
in their dormer rooms

        eternal banishment

Who are usually grateful
to anyone who prevents them
from taking a false step

And having reached the summit
would like to stay there
even if the stairs are withdrawn

Originally published in The Blue Stairs *(New York: Corinth Books, 1968).*
Note: The Modern Museum in Amsterdam has blue stairs.

The Shadow of Surrealism

I grew up under the shadow of Surrealism. In that creative atmosphere of magical rites there was no recognized separation between the arts. Those of us who shared this atmosphere brightened by Apollinaire, Éluard, Valéry, Breton, considered ourselves part of a hemisphere where all the arts evolved around one another, a central plaza with roads which led from palette to quill to clef. One could never again look at poetry as a locked kingdom. Poetry extended vertically, as well as horizontally. Never was it motionless within a linear structure. Assisting in this poetic mobility would be an associative art within whose eye the poet might gaze for reassurance, and for a glowing impersonal empathy.

We have read of the relation of Gertrude Stein to Picasso. She saw her own work and Cubist painting as engaged in a similar struggle. She even went so far as to write Cubist portraits. What actually she was seeking was an escape from literature, or from "the literary." She saw and envied the freedom shared by Picasso, Braque, and Gris and their breakthrough from formalism to Cubism. Painters are the revolutionaries to whom writers turn in their desire to break from the solemnity of the judicious rules of their craft.

During the explosive era of Abstract-Expressionism we not only admired the work of painters breaking rules of art performing on the canvas the otherwise concealed, emotional state of the painter, we became envious of the activity of their personal lives.

This may be taken by a few as a frivolous remark, but the remark contains a metaphor in which the natural gravity of life is replaced by the gratification of secret desires. Art as reflection becomes more instantaneous, willful, enthusiastic, freed by action. Painters naturally gravitate toward expensive cars, lofts and chateaux, urged by the prices affixed to their art.

Money, fame pursue painters with a frequency that stuns the poet. Just as the extravagance of painters is admired, so is their ability to leap the boundaries of experiment applauded by their market. In a similar situation of leaping boundaries of experiment, the poet is frowned upon by the academies from which financial reward is infrequently extended.

Some poets even desire to sit under umbrellas at Mougins with Picasso or share a villa.

As a poet who happened to be employed by an art journal, I was exposed to the temperament caused by the explosion of Abstract-Expressionism, and my personal relationships with its painters certainly influenced the way I observed both nature and the book. I have always believed in a direct heritage shared by Frank O'Hara and Apollinaire, perhaps a deliberately decided one. O'Hara was very close in sensibility to the French poets of Cubism. He described the process of Abstract-Expressionism far more closely than any critic or art historian in his poem "Why I Am Not a Painter."

The measure by which one art form works upon another is explained by Rilke in his book *The Art of Cézanne*. I was startled in this book to find a description of my response to painting. Rilke tells us that he was interested in Cézanne because he wanted to find out how the painter worked *so that he might apply Cézanne's discoveries to his own work.*

I confess that often when looking at art I do not ask what it means, or how was the paint applied, the color chosen, but what has led the artist into this particular situation, what permits this particular piece of work, and how is it solved. When I look at certain paintings they begin to enter my unconscious. I then ask how the metamorphosis took place, and if the process I witness can be used in my own work. An explanation of process is what Rilke asked of Cézanne. He did not question what Cézanne meant to him, he wanted to *borrow his method from the master.*

I admired a painting of Matisse of a bowl of goldfish. I put a poster of this painting on my wall and looked at it daily. I began to realize very slowly that this great sensualist was also an intellectual manipulator of space who misled us by his concentration on color. How he created his sensual interiors was a solemn intellectual problem. I was then working on a poem whose ostensible subject was three bodies of water: a pond, a swimming pool and the sea. Giving the poem a title, "Water Kingdoms," I submitted it to a magazine and the poem was rejected.

With a sidelong look at the Matisse goldfish on the wall, I began to reconsider the poem. In the Matisse poster, the goldfish are placed in their bowl on a table. The table appears in another Matisse painting owned by the Museum of Modern Art. It is called *The Rose Marble Table.* I had cherished a fondness for this painting and had attached it to my life. Now I began to consider the table. I became more intimate with the painting and progress of Matisse. The poem is called "The Rose Marble Table."

Once I sublet an apartment overlooking Union Square. I came to dislike the cold north light of the apartment and I admit I was unhappy while I lived there. However, the owner's library included several books on Kandinsky. There was one book that quoted him on the necessity in art for an "inner sound." To me, this is the essential "noise" of poetry. Another book showed photographs of Kandinsky's Moscow apartment. The artist, his ideas, and his dwelling place became a solace to me.

One day looking down on Union Square from the apartment, the sudden realization arrived that Union Square looked remarkably like the Moscow park seen from Kandinsky's apartment.

Several years passed and I moved near the south side of Union Square. I walked over to Union Square one day and looked up at my former apartment. The building now seemed to resemble the old photograph of Kandinsky's apartment. That evening I began to write a poem about the last evening Kandinsky had spent in Moscow before going into exile. I called the poem "The View from Kandinsky's Window."

From a talk given at the Kouros Gallery, New York City, 1986. Previously published in the Pen American Center Newsletter, No. 2, 1987, *and in* Women's Studies, *vol. 30, no. 1, a special issue on Barbara Guest as "The Shadow of Surrealism"; Catherine Kasper, editor. "The Rose Marble Table" and "The View from Kandinsky's Window" were published in* Fair Realism (*Los Angeles: Sun & Moon Press, 1989*).

Walter Benjamin in a Museum

from his Moscow Diary

IT SEEMED TO ME THAT TO THE EXTENT THAT ONE
GRASPS A PAINTING, ONE DOES NOT IN ANY WAY ENTER
INTO ITS SPACE. RATHER, THIS SPACE THRUSTS ITSELF
FORWARD, ESPECIALLY IN VARIOUS VERY SPECIFIC SPOTS.

IT OPENS UP TO US IN CORNERS AND ANGLES IN WHICH
WE BELIEVE WE CAN LOCALIZE CRUCIAL EXPERIENCES
OF THE PAST: THERE IS SOMETHING INEXPLICABLY
FAMILIAR ABOUT THESE SPOTS.

THE SAME OBSERVATION IS TRUE OF THE LITERARY LIFE. READING IS
NOT THE EQUIVALENT OF EXPLANATION. (GUEST)

POUND MIGHT HAVE OBSERVED TO HIM:

"ALL EFFORTS TO MAKE POLITICS AESTHETIC ONLY CULMINATE IN
WAR."[1]

IN THE PROCESS EVERYTHING CHANGED FOR BENJAMIN. IN HIS THOUGHTS IT WAS AS IF HE HAD TAKEN THE WATER COLOR AND GOUACHE OF A DREAM.

HE MOUNTED IT ON CARDBOARD.
THIS WAS HIS ESSAY. MOLDED NOW AFTER PAINTING. HE HAD CARDBOARD. THUS WAS HIS ESSAY NOW TRULY AFTER PAINTING. HE HAD LOST HIS ORIGINAL SCHEME. THE PHILOSOPHER USURPED BY A PRIVATE DREAM.

———————

Born in Berlin of upper-class Jewish parentage, Walter Benjamin, essayist and man of letters, has become one of the legends of the twentieth century. Fearful of the Gestapo, he committed suicide at the Spanish border, where he had planned his escape.

1 John Tytell, Ezra Pound: The Solitary Volcano *(New York: Doubleday, 1987).*

Poetic Creation

In reaching for this flower "absent from all bouquets,"
we are in the singular field of poetic creation.

The roots of this absent flower are located in Symbolism.
The reader must prepare to accept Symbolism as the
bartered Bride of Modernism.

Imagism

The Image can be of two sorts. It can arise in the mind. It is then 'subjective.' External causes play upon the mind, perhaps emerge, if so they are drawn into the mind, fused, transmitted, and emerge in an Image unlike themselves. Secondly, the Image can be objective. Emotion seizing up some external scene or action carries it intact to the mind; and that vortex purges it of all save the essential or dominant or dramatic qualities, and it emerges like the external original. In either case the Image is more than an idea. It is a vortex or cluster of fused ideas and is endowed with energy. If it does not fulfill these specifications, it is not what I mean by an image.

—Ezra Pound, "Affirmations (as for *Imagisme*),"
The New Age, 1915

One day in those early days, Pound himself had looked upon those crossing a bridge over the Seine and written:

The apparition of these faces in the crowd;
Petals on a wet, black bough

Imagism has arrived! Henri Bergson in Paris said: image is a locus between intuition and concept.

In London, Hulme, a friend of Pound, was also exploring the image for a new kind of Impressionism. Then Pound was back in Provence writing what could be called, in later days, a form of the *Cantos*. The former impressionism was moved into a new form.

> The wind came, and the rain
> And the mist gathered about the trees in the valley.

Pound was writing very modern verse. It would be exchanged for *The Cantos*.

In London H.D. was writing Imagist verse.

Modernism presenting itself.

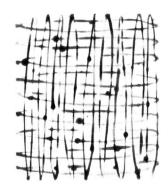

H.D. and the Conflict of Imagism

I am going to read from the chapter "H.D. Imagiste" in my biography of
H.D. I shall do so because I believe that the scene I describe is well-staged.
I use those words carefully. I am not satisfied with this scene, although I
have reported it. It plays remarkably like the first act of a drama, as I suppose it is. The figure of Richard Aldington is missing. But we have it here
in all its bright clothing, a dramatic meeting between two protagonists who
would affect one another for a lifetime and the introduction of a poetics
that would for ten years affect the direction of H.D.'s poetry and give per-
manent luster to her name as an Imagist:

> It is September 1912, a year after Hilda arrived in Europe. She
> has been at the British Museum studying the Greek friezes
> and plates of Egyptian figures. She is abstracted, contempla-
> tive. And yet there is a purposeful air about her as she hur-
> ries down the museum steps to the nearby museum bun
> shop. Ezra Pound is waiting there for her. He is dressed in his
> Whistlerian garb, the velvet jacket, the loose tie. Together
> they are a pictorial couple. She is so tall and lean, beautiful
> with the squared jaw and the hair falling over her brow. He
> is certainly no ordinary clerk. His reddish hair is long and
> tumbled, he has a watchful impudent look about the eyes.
> Something of that air of inquisitive fantasy Aubrey Beards-
> ley used to catch in his drawings. Neither at this moment is
> interested in appearances. There is a more direct reason for
> the meeting. Hilda has consented to show Ezra Pound her
> new poems.

She puts her books and gloves onto a chair, takes out a notebook, and hands it to him.

He reads "Hermes of the Ways." Hilda's poem had been suggested by an invocation to Hermes by the poetess Anyte that was in the Greek Anthology Pound has introduced her to.

"Why, Dryad, this is good!"

He takes out a sharp red pencil, changes a word here or there, crosses one out. He rereads the poem, and then the next one, "Acon," another poem based on a translation from a Latin Renaissance book he had also given her. Then there is "Orchard." Pound is really pleased. She is a model pupil. More than that, she is a poet; the scornful, exacting teacher is now certain of this. Selecting "Hermes of the Ways," and giving her one of his catlike looks, he again takes up his pencil and signs the poem: "H.D. Imagiste."

That is the story. The attitudes, the gestures, the theatricality are in character. It is a brilliant coup. Pound has created another poet, acolyte. He has added a disciple to the new ism he is about to create and introduce to the market.

Would that today the excised poem with its corrections might rest in the Berg Collection in New York, alongside Pound's similar selective corrections and deletions to "The Waste Land" of Eliot.[1]

And now I will tell you one of the reasons why I am not satisfied with this setting. Aldington, Pound and H.D. had been in Paris at the same time, in 1912. Paris was the center of Modernism. Of Cubism, Impressionism, Simultaneousism, Symbolism, which would be overtaken by Imagism. The preparation for Pound's doctrine of *Imagisme* must have taken place in Paris, and been discussed in his lodgings in London over the previous months.

In the bun shop we have a fairytale setting where the magician waves his wand and anoints the poet. The poems were in her handbag. Did she show them to Pound expecting he would write Imagiste after them?

Perhaps it was the other way around. Pound needed the poetry of H.D. to launch *Imagisme*. Were those poems of H.D. inspired by that remarkable new poem, "The Return," written by Pound, a poem Pound may have considered his first venture into Imagism?

Whatever may be the truth we know that Pound was determined Imagism initiate the poetry of the future. He did not want H.D. or himself to remain unrecognized, "living under the staircase, where all must pass him and no one pays any attention to him. . . ."[2] Not Pound the master-magician nor his protégée.

As I wrote in my biography, I wish that the poems she showed Pound that day with his corrections were in a library, as "The Waste Land" is in the Berg Library. We might see for ourselves Pound's editing of "Hermes of the Ways," "Acon," and "Orchard."

In 1915 in "Affirmations," Pound wrote:

The Image can be of two sorts. It can arise within the mind. It is then 'subjective.' External causes play upon the mind, perhaps; if so they are drawn into the mind, fused, transmitted, and emerge in an Image unlike themselves. Secondly, the Image can be objective. Emotion seizing up some external scene or action carries it intact to the mind; and that vortex purges it of all save the essential or dominant or dramatic qualities, and it emerges like the external original. In either case the Image is more than an idea. It is a vortex or cluster of fused ideas and is endowed with energy. If it does not fulfill these specifications, it is not what I mean by an Image.[3]

This is three years after the meeting in the bun shop. Meanwhile Pound, briefly engaged with the Vorticists, had not abandoned Imagism for Vorticism. Vorticism, he came to realize, was for painters. However, he made clear to Harriet Monroe regarding his own translations that he was determined "to break the surface of convention."

H.D. was beginning her own struggle with what Williams in "Asphodel" calls "the tyranny of the image" (wonderful phrase). Pound had firmly stressed that you did not work up to the image—no reflections, hesitations, equivocation, hints. The image strikes once with its full force—and brilliantly, "it occurs in an instant."

Although her poetry shows that she assimilated in her own way many of Pound's affirmations, I don't believe the program or the vision instinct in Pound's concept of Imagism ever in detail or magnitude penetrated the poetics H.D. evolved for herself.

Essentially she used the movement as a wheel for her own poetry. She was at this time an instinctual poet. She had a small definite vocabulary of words ("shell," "garden," "flower") into which she fitted a Greek landscape with Greek figures. That is, she narrowed the concept of Imagism. To those today who do not accept the genius of Pound's drive to change, to alter, above all to achieve a modern scheme of poetics that accompanied Cubism and Joyce's *Ulysses,* that evolved a poetry of Modernism, she is known as the "purest" Imagist of them all.

H.D.'s translations "invent" a method of translation that incorporates her own exceptional ear. In her adaptation of Euripides' ION we find a sophisticated use of imagistic poetics. Yet it is a performance. *Hippolytus Temporizes* is an extraordinary example of H.D.'s use of Imagism. The whole mood of the play, based on the Greek myth, completed in

1927 and partly inspired by a play of Euripides, reflects her use of the spatial techniques of Imagism. A use which she arrives at in her poetry only when the poetry is fragmented.

The form she has chosen architecturally expands the technique. In this play exist some of her loveliest, most startling effects.

In her poetry, H.D.'s conception of Imagism was of the poem taking place in a much smaller, defined space, a tighter space than Pound conceived. This is why later she wanted to write more "open" poetry. Her later attitude could perhaps be explained by the words of a reviewer of the *Imagist Anthology* who wrote:

> It is always the Imagist's danger that in his statement of facts of form, colour and sensuous impression, he may miss that further vision that may not be confined in exact language which the true poet always suggests to us.

(Note the pronoun "he" throughout. In defense, however, even we can only say "she" regarding the one female Imagist before the Amygist.) I should like to suggest now that we entertain another idea; that is, we consider the situation of Eliot, Pound and H.D. as exiles or expatriates (to use a more polite word, but one shunned by James Joyce). By choice and selectivity they are isolated from their native country.

Imagism concerns itself with the isolation of the image. The momentum of the poem flows toward the suddenness of the image. This suddenness, this overflowing of an image into space, out of nowhere, is purposeful. All of this energy is employed to give definition to the poem; to gather up the particulars, the threads, the hints of what is being said into a summation or a description, a sudden alarming or beneficent but immediate summation of what the poem has been all about. We are dealing with time and with space and movement. There must be nothing, finally, lying around inert. Yet the image despite all its energy and activity has arrived as if it were a foreign substance. It is strangely isolated. This isolation or foreignness of the image from the rest of the poem exerts a fascination to which the poem is willing to submit, but not always the reader. The reader is apt to say, "oh, another image," or "oh, another picture"—remember that Imagism is highly pictorial and visual. If you consider this, you realize the image has a lonely perch.

At the same time we must also recognize that these three Americans in Europe, together with their counterparts in America, Williams and Stevens, formed the background of the modernist movement as we know it today. (I am going to suggest that Stevens himself, the executive of an insurance company, was just as much isolated in Hartford, Connecticut. That dwelling in the inner sanctum of his home in which he received nobody, sitting in a small garden sipping wine and eating cheese without conversation even with his wife, he maintained the embrace of exile.) I shall not include Williams because, despite Pound's insistence on Williams's Spanish ancestry, he was at home in New Jersey. The embrace of exile and the disease of exile accompanied Eliot, Pound, and H.D. throughout their lives.

In exile there is freedom, also. Freedom to maneuver, freedom to adopt a persona. And freedom, in particular, to use a language in whatever context you wish. Language is private. Language speaks your language. I don't wish to argue that Pound's insistence on Imagism could not have happened in America, although I believe this is true. I conjecture that his exile, his formal isolation into which entered Wyndham Lewis, Ford Madox Ford, and Yeats, minds of such a degree he could not have encountered in the America he knew, assisted him in his concentration and formulation of Imagism, even the escape from Imagism, briefly, into Vorticism, so that finally in the isolation of Rapallo he was able to refine its principles for his own uses.

D.H. Lawrence rationalized that Imagism "comes from the American psyche, which might, were it not fed the artistry of the poets, have turned into as mindless a poetry as the Futurists produced."

Certainly H.D., who revelled in her new freedom in England, was willing to listen to the dictates of her compatriot. He was explaining the country of the imagination and articulated the power of poetry, and surrounded by such a balustrade she was protected from loneliness, lent strength to cope with the self-questioning that comes to expatriates.

When Pound in 1912 wrote about H.D.'s work to Harriet Monroe seeking publication for H.D.'s poetry, he was not afraid to rely on the civilizing influence of expatriatism.

> This is the sort of American stuff that I can show here and in Paris without its being ridiculed. Objective — no slither: direct — no excessive use of adjectives, no metaphors that won't permit examination. It's straight talk, straight as the Greek![4]

"Straight as the Greek" is purposeful historicism to Monroe in Chicago.

And it is well to remember that in pre–World War America there was a Victorian America struggling to rid itself of confining ideologies, but still struggling, still gripped in a stronger vise of poetics than was British poetry. British poetry was something to come to grips with. It was a force. An inherited force. One could say the name Swinburne and it had value, it had probity beyond romance; an American could recognize in Swinburne the beginning of a beginning. In America poetry was largely ornament and moralism. The pictorial images contained no shafts of light.

There was no Symbolism to alter and appropriate into Imagism as Poussin was changed into nature, the nature of Cubism.

For H.D., once she had become a high-priestess of Imagism, a new struggle began. The struggle with the domination of the image would come later. This other conflict was with the force, the energy, and the persona of Pound himself.

"Toward the Piraeus," published in *Heliodora* in 1924, is directed forbiddingly at Pound, with its beginning line "You would have broken my wings":

> It was not chastity that made me wild, but fear
> that my weapon, tempered in different heat;
> was over-matched by yours, and your hand
> skilled to yield death-blows, might break
>
> With the slightest turn — no ill will meant —
> my own lesser, yet still somewhat fine-wrought,
> fiery-tempered, delicate, over-passionate steel.[5]

This is a very explicit statement and with the high edge of steel she was informing him that her poetry might turn against his rule, his might, that she would indeed find another source. Pound would write "brutally," so H.D. thought, about *Hedylus* which followed *Heliodora*. In *Hedylus* she attempts to evoke the spirit of the woman poet, Hedyle. H.D. later admitted that *Hedylus* is a retelling of her own story in a classical setting. It may be a clumsy attempt to deal with a Greek environment, but we are astounded that Pound warned Circe "to get out of her pig-sty." Pound is no longer interested in, nor did he approve of, her dependence on Greek subject matter.

In her memoir of Pound, *End To Torment* (a title Pound would call "optimistic"), written while Pound was in St. Elizabeth's, and H.D. more pleasantly incarcerated in a clinic at Kusnacht, Switzerland, she wrote: "Ezra would have destroyed me and the Air and Crystal of my poetry."

Pound may at the time have been infuriated by the publisher's blurb on the Jonathan Cape edition of *Heliodora and Other Poems.*

"Her work blends European suavity with a kind of red-Indian terseness, nerve and barbarity of phrase." A more deliberately inaccurate description of one of her most selective books could scarcely have been printed.

Pound would several years later come in for some of that barbarity himself. Max Beerbohm in Rapallo remarked to Phyllis Bottome that Pound "seemed out of place here. I should prefer to watch him in the primeval forests of his native land wielding an axe against some giant tree. Could you not persuade him to return to a country in which there is more room?"

The *Collected Poems* of 1925 summed up H.D.'s Imagist phase. This is a wonderful book. Eighty-eight pages of pure H.D. Imagism. It begins with "Sea Garden," followed by "The Helmsman," "Sea Lily," "The Gift," "Sea Poppies," "Hermes of the Ways" — a powerful, near-perfect poem, "Orchard." The youthful H.D. is here, her poems so carefully formed, delicate with sturdy stems. Of course the theme is minor with too much sand, wind, wave, no wonder she wanted to spread out her wings and she wanted also to celebrate the hermetic world. But here the scene is filled with light. And so is the combination of Imagism and myth of these poems. And the knowledge that the poet is in secure control of her craft. The doctrines of Imagism gave her this hold on her poetry. "Hard light, clear edges."

The late work of H.D., *Hermetic Definition* and *Helen in Egypt,* are another H.D. She has entered another place; she is reaching for the tools of the unconscious.

Adalaide Morris has called H.D. Imagist, Clairvoyant, Cinemastic, Prophetic. Imagist survives as a subsidiary in the contemplated frame of her work.

Rid of the tyranny of the image, H.D.'s new discovery is the power of narrative form. This is followed by improvisation — actually free association with words and sound: "Marah," "Mar," "Mer," etc. However, her old Imagist training that taught her to avoid the superfluous word would still inhibit her from total submission to the apocalyptic speech she would surrender to in her World War II period.

Imagism provided discipline, even if she wanted to throw out its bathwater.

Then in 1956 H.D. made a celebrated visit to Yale. She was interviewed by the *New Haven Register* whose lead article was headed "Poet Hilda Doolittle on Yale Visit Assails Imagist Label Used to Describe Her Work." The paper reported that H.D. denounced the label. She emphasized that the term could not be applied to describe her work written since World War II.

H.D. then continued to say, "I don't know that labels matter very much. One writes the kind of poetry one likes. Other people put labels on it." In its own way this is a true statement, if not true to what she specifically refers. Pound had indeed "labeled" the poem she had shyly showed him in the tearoom.

When asked what was meant by Imagism, she answered, "Something that was important for poets learning their craft early in this century. It is still important to any poet learning his craft. But after learning his craft, the poet will find his true direction, as I hope I have."

We, however, know that she was vastly indebted to the Imagist movement. Her renown had come through her association with the movement and her designation as the "purest" Imagist of them all. (Purest if not the greatest. It is my belief that *The Cantos* are the great affirmation of Imagism.) By then Imagism as a literary term had entered literary history. Aldington decried Imagism in a letter to her. Now it was H.D.'s turn to be more gentle in her response toward Imagism. When she answered his letter she wrote: "How sad I am that you so dislike having to do with the Imagist sign. I have been bored with it, too. But at seventy-two it is part of my youth."

At this age she had just completed "Helen in Egypt." She believed that the early H.D., the poet of the *Collected Poems* of 1925, had matured with this later book and she believed Imagism was too microscopic a term for her later work, which had moved into narrative which she believed was freer, more discursive, more philosophical, more grown-up in dealing with the passions of the world, and which dwelt both in myth and in the immediate contemporary world.

What is noticeable in the late work are the traces of real struggle inside and outside the levels of obedience to form. A move in direct opposition to Pound's "language is made of concrete things."

Her later poetry resorted to a repetitive discursive style whose passages are filled with the esotericism that preoccupied her thoughts. She now used a longer explosive line interrupted by shorter broken lines. The effect is of interior monologue in search of a subject that once found is held up to us like a Medusa head. The poems are instructive, not descriptive as in her Imagistic work.

She came to rely on an emotive reaction to Christian and esoteric orthodoxy in her late poetry. Yet within the form, the shape of her poetry, is a rebellion from the orthodoxy not only of Imagism, but of any formal poetics. She became a law unto herself.

The war trilogy maintains the intensity apparent in her early poems without the control that Imagism demanded. When she abandoned the form of Imagism she abandoned many of its precepts, except Pound's rule against use of "ornament." Her poems are never ornamental and, with all her use of Greek location, there is no archaicism, there are no "quaint devices" of the sort Pound warned about in *Lustra*.

The *Trilogy* poems to me are comparable to the war poems of Edith Sitwell. H.D. speaks in the overtones of Moravianism, of Christianity, although her poetry is more religious than Sitwell's appeal to the pagan. H.D. is both more allusive and more complicated. Yet the sound is similarly alerting, the same effect of high emotion is there. A similar note of authority.

In *The Cantos* of Pound, although the pattern of words on his page seems loose or open, the poems move on many levels of thought; ideas are superimposed above images or images precede ideas. There is order and direction within the multi-dimensional effect of his poetry that derives from Imagism.

"The body is inside the soul," Pound said. We can transpose these words to read: *the body of the work is inside the image.*

When H.D. deliberately turned away from the Imagist principles it can be surmised that she wished her work to expand both poetically and emotionally. Enclosure was what she feared most; being inside a given set of rules was becoming anathema to her. Had she not said early on "I am not a Theorist"? The womb-like claustrophobia of the image both in the poem, and the weight of it on herself as the persona for this invention of Pound, were becoming an affliction.

Her life had taken other turns. "There was an H.D. before the War," as she often said, and there was by 1925 another H.D. It is eighty years since the staged meeting in the tea shop. And today Imagism has entered our literary history, has become an accessory to our skills.

Searching again into the mystery of H.D., her role in literature as an Imagist, and reading the distinctly non-imagistic body of her late work, perhaps we can believe she was in search of the "deep truth" that Shelley in *Prometheus Unbound* declares is "imageless."

Read at the Voice Box Royal Festival Hall in London, April 26, 1992,
in celebration of the "Centennial of Imagism." Published in SAGETRIEB,
vol. 15, nos. 1 and 3, Spring and Fall, 1996; Burton Hatlen, editor.

1 *Barbara Guest,* Herself Defined: The Poet H.D. and Her World *(New York: Brill, 1984).*

2 *Hugo von Hofmannsthal,* The Poet of Our Time.

3 *Ezra Pound, "Affirmations (as for imagisme)," in* The New Age, *January 28, 1915.*

4 *Ezra Pound,* Selected Letters of Ezra Pound 1907–1941; *D.D. Paige, editor (New York: Faber and Faber, 1950).*

5 *H.D.,* Collected Poems 1912–1944 *(New York: New Directions, 1992).*

An Inconsiderate Preface

Someone spoke on the stairway in Spanish, another answered in Italian. There must have been a reasonable communication as the conversation ended in laughter.

The combined languages as she listened formed a third which might have been, with its rasp, Portuguese. In her former apartment house that language was heard in hallways and near the elevator. It belonged to the super and his relatives who, recently immigrated, spread the language like pieces of broken pottery. The super had an air about him she could not locate. Once she had visited Lisbon which reminded her, with the cold winds and clear air, of San Francisco, the physical prominence of hills. This identification may have interrupted her interest in the local speech. She did not listen to the language, letting it hang beside her, as if in a sling. In New York its flutter teased her. She wrote to a friend that Portuguese was rough, not smooth like jasper or porphyry.

Lately she had concentrated on the work of Tommaso Landolfi and it was while reading a translation of *Words in Commotion* that she overheard her landlady and the tenant conversing on the stairway. Made restless by their commotive sounds she turned to another translation. Literature was bequeathing her a second ear, like factory noise next door. Her ear began to ache with minute figures etched by translation.

In the translator Helen Caldwell's preface to *Helena* by the Brazilian writer Machado de Assis there is an apology for other translations of his work. Several of those books she had read and admired, especially the one with the difficult title combining a dog and a philosopher. A novel of "experiment," or a novel taking experimental exits was the only way de Assis could explain the reality of literary isolation.

Helena, "not a major novel," was written in 1853 and she was urged to regard it as a "romantic novel" or a "novel of romance." What surprised the translator was how this tag embarrassed the author who was astonished when by 1873 *Helena* "had reached a vast audience."

"Romantic" words appearing in the text were noted to prove how mistaken de Assis had been in rejecting his title to romance. *Human hearts, love, feelings, soul, anguish, honor, longing,* are strung together like ripe valentines.

Annoyed by the inconsiderate preface she determined to make her own list of the *themes* of *Helena*, a practice she had discarded when leaving school. She found that outlines, or *themes* increased the monumentality of George Eliot or Dostoevsky and spun out their interminable greatness. Besides, these *themes* usually concealed the true temperament of the novel.

1. the restrictions of society on women

She began with this subject because she had found in the translated *Correspondence* of Berthe Morisot similar restrictions suffered by the artist, a victim of her middle-class milieu, that prevented her from attending the brothels of Lautrec, embracing the nude models of Degas, participating in the evenings of Mallarmé, or even entering a cafe. These severe limitations not only affected her art but, like the fate of Helena, were perhaps responsible for an early death hastened by impotent rage.

2. the Catholic church

Does de Assis imply that the exemplary yet destructive priest was in love with Helena? The activities of the priest belie his sweetened authority.

3. the position of slaves

"Slaves like to go on errands, because it is the only time they can be alone." De Assis, the son of freed slaves, chooses a slave as the innocent catalyst of his "family's" destruction.

4. incest

Friends who wish him to do them a favor sidle up to the brother and whisper, "You know I am terribly fond of your sister." The sister, when accused of being passionately in love with a person other than her fiancé, "blushed furiously." How differently this theme in Thomas Mann's *The Blood of the Walsungs*, a story of incest between twins, affects us. The colonial story of de Assis breathes less heavily than the German. It is soothing, almost idyllic.

She was distressed by her earlier neglect of the masterful diversions concealing from readers the real purposes of de Assis. She felt foolish for having been taken in by the translator's dubiety that withheld the lash of de Assis, his pretense of writing a sorrowful story of thwarted passion while his attention is placed elsewhere: the exposure of society's appetite.

The list pleased her. She experienced the serenity that comes when one gains control through a discipline. She refreshed herself with a small bottle of grapefruit juice. The juice brought to mind the acrid wind that blows through the novels, relieved by the gentleness with which de Assis attaches himself to the countryside beyond Rio de Janeiro. There, nature in the sensitive embrace of de Assis eludes the modelling of a translator.

The Beautiful Voyage

To arrange its dimensions the poem stretches (looking outwardly and inwardly), thus obtaining a plasticity that the flat, the basic words, what we call "the language of a poem," demand, and further, depend on.

This cannot be achieved through language alone, but arrives from tensions placed on the Structure: variability of meter, fleeting moods of expression, mutability of consonants and vowels.

Respect your private language.

Context is a logical emergence (even "emergency" inside) from inside the poem.

And "stretches the imagination without disabling it."

Plasticity, strive for noble Plasticity.

Never "negotiate" with the reader by projecting the reader's aims into the poem, such as a "desirable subject."

Poet and reader perform together on a high wire strung over a platform between their *separated selves.*

Tension between the poem and the poet creates an empathy/
this tension relies on and *alters the plasticity of poetic language.*

A poem stretches when Pressure on a word causes the poem to stretch. Go to the poem, observe, see if the word is consistent within the poem — never desert meaning for a word.

the special circumstances within which it makes sense
    circumstances upon which it is used.

You enter the poem like Ulysses embarking on a "beautiful voyage."

The rules are inside your head.   They belong to you.   As you grow along with poetry you learn there are certain things the tribe cannot do (not rules) and you cannot do if you are to maintain your best position within the poem.

When in trouble depend upon imagination.

Picasso, when facing his inquisitors: "Subject matter? You have to have an idea of what you are going to do, but it should be a vague idea."

To translate this sensitive remark (to my way of thinking): the poem should not be programmatic, or didactic, or show-off.   But another way is to go inside the poem itself and   *be in the dark*   at the beginning of the journey. Here, with a vague idea (as Picasso suggested) of what to write,

    and I am *trembling*   am trembling with the excitement

      This trembling is a good idea, because it means
you are not exactly in charge. Ulysses learned, to his dismay and once to his delight,

      his ship would encounter circumstances   *well beyond his control*
Magic and spells   *would victimize*   poetry entering its own domain
    may (for a time) cast its spell over the poet

you, also, are going to *entertain within the poem circumstances over which*
you must eventually take control, but at first you have no control

if you are a good poet to begin with you have an idea and you know enough
      about where your objectives are, but someone here allows
the poem's powers, even as magic entered the sails of Ulysses, and not by
      didacticism of your own will   *as you enter the great seas or*
          little bay of your poem.

what Picasso said about subject matter:
"It's always something else in the end."

While the poem is in the making it changes as thoughts change. There are certain rhythmical tides and swells on this voyage when the poem gains control of its shape and enters its own rhythmical waters; times when the poem withdraws into itself/ and as you coast 'musing' remember the rocks upon which the Sirens sang . . . .

when the poem can be, I believe, in most danger.

What is so fascinating about poetry is: how many encounters we meet with on the way of its writing.

And the explicit will of the poem, until it releases.   the myth: of itself

"the poem wrote itself." *when the identity of the poem is so fixed the poem is willing to trust itself to the poet.*

before the poem can "write itself"

amid currents: "reality" and multi-identificational
objectives / Body, Mind, Soul /

the dark identity of a poem must be encountered

Consider

CONSIDER

    DIFFERENT PLANS ONE

HAS FOR A POEM.

SURPRISE THE POEM OFFERS—

BEHIND THE WEATHERED DOOR

    NOSTALGIA OF THE INFINITE—

    DE CHIRICO.

Mysteriously Defining the Mysterious:
Byzantine Proposals of Poetry

We once took a ship from Beirut and sailed along the coast of Turkey, to Byzantium. The ship on which we sailed first anchored in the harbor of the Turkish town Mersan. We dropped anchor near a Russian freighter, and there were all the signs of excitement on our ship of nearness to the enemy stranger. But we were curious about this port and left ship entering the sandy town we believed only offered a few trees, an oasis.

Lo! as we walked further into the town we found there was a bazaar, an open bazaar, unlike the covered bazaars of Morocco and Damascus. Perhaps a simple place where country people brought their stuffs, as they had in Hardy's *Jude the Obscure*. And the objective of these country folk was to sell their wares in Mersan. There were a few harborside attempts at a modern world in the cafes with their umbrellas, but little else appeared until we walked further into the town.

We were in an open square. Before us were laid golden, silken stuffs of such serious and sophisticated spinning and weaving only to be exhibited in the expensive shops of the West. Palatial silks, subtle in color and meaning. Silks tumbling out of baskets, one could not believe the dust lying at our feet: were they after all simple folk who offered these goods in the bazaar?

The poet listening to the silk hears the singing of birds. I took home the rare silk. The silk was turned into curtains and began to lead a domestic existence, its history asleep, much as a poem enters into an anthology. (Who knows when those Mersan curtains rustled and their sound entered my poetry.)

This experience in Mersan may be called a first encounter with the Byzantine. Underneath the surface of the poem there is the presence of "the something else." Mallarmé said, "Not the thing, but its effect." The "effect" is what I have been leading to with my curtains from Mersan. The "thing" is the poetic process which lends its "effect" (the silk of the curtains) to the poem. Process and effect, each go about in disguise. They must be uncovered, these other realms Keats discovered "When First Looking into Chapman's Homer."

Reading Poe, we discover that "things are not what they seem to be." This discovery was introduced to us earlier by Shakespeare where the actors wear disguise, or their true identity is hidden even from them. In *Twelfth Night* the actor whispers, "Things are not what they seem to be."

Mallarmé and Baudelaire conscientiously introduce this concept into poetry, thereby adding another dimension to exceed the use of symbol. "Not the thing, but the effect it produces." This effect lends a labyrinthine element to the statement of a poem. It is necessary to follow a circuitous path into the realms of literature.

Stevens called a poem "a finikin thing of air." At its beginning, a poem floats on thin air until it is bolstered in its flight by "a purple bird" that shares the extravagance of being rare. His is a Byzantine way of entering a poem, to call it a piece of air, to let it sing, then to conclude it is rare.

In whatever disguise reality becomes visible to the poet, there is the choice of withdrawing from it visibility to create a secret life. The poem is the unburdening of ghosts of the past who have come to haunt the writer exposed to the labyrinth. These are ghosts not words; they are the ephemera that surround and decorate the mind of the poet, a halo rescued from life. And it is the poet's halo that we see arching within the poem, not the full dress of rhyme or structure. Not the artifice of landscape or the surround of language. Shelley liked to think of spirits hid in a cloud, and Byzantine poets imagined genies escaping from familiar earthenware bottles, and Blake drew angels. Mandelstam heard the inner sound "spilling into his fingers."

Kandinsky writes that "a problem all art imposes is the evaluation of its distance from its source." And it is within the convoluted travel to the dramatic center that we trace the spirituality within Kandinsky's painting. He also had a concept of "inner sound," a sound that intimidates the creative condition of the artist and controls the temperament of the painting. He writes, "every 'vibration' that urges communication to arrive out of 'inner necessity', every element should be creatively inserted in the work in order to *evoke that inner sound, the noise of the imagination.*" The rustle of silk in Mersan evoked the noise of the imagination.

Imagination is the spirit inside the poem, a nostalgia for the infinite, louder than silk.

The inner sound of the poet protects the poet. Delacroix wrote that painters of marine life do not represent the sea satisfactorily. "They want to show too much science, make portraits of waves, as landscape artists make portraits of trees." His argument is that these seascapes do not concern themselves with the effect on the imagination, they are absorbed by details, "turning the mind away." Tending to this detail, the artist whose sole urgency is his subject matter neglects the depth rendered by Imagination.

———

First appeared in HOW(ever) *vol. 3, no. 3 (San Francisco: October, 1986); Kathleen Fraser, editor. Also published in* Jubilat, *Fall 2002; Peter Gizzi, editor.*

Vision and Mundanity

Vision is conjoined to the poet's spiritual life, of which the poem itself is a résumé. The "spirit" or the "vision" of a poem arises from the contents of the poet's unconscious. The poet directs this "spillover" into the poem.

Perhaps while considering a projected poem the poet becomes rapt in a vision, which is like a hood over the head. Life as it appears—or an object or landscape as they appear on the lens of this apparitional hood—become so magnetic their energy is directed into a poem. As closely as possible the poet wishes to align the contents of the subject matter with that vision of the subject.

It seems possible that words may occur in a fixed space and sequence so they can be called "words of a poem." We may then say the poem is made of words. And it is true that many poems are constructed solely of words. These are the words that sit on paper without vision.

The place where vision should glow in a poem may also be occupied by ideas. These ideas, unless proceeding from vision, are the utensils of words. Inorganic, they preempt the shape of vision.

Words without vision are deprived of stability. They cling desperately to a mirrored surface in an effort to attach themselves to a surface because they have no direction and no stabilized vocation. They become furtive, thirsty for a version of themselves that contains no failure of vision. Words contain their own beauty of face, but they desire an occupation. They cannot exist on beauty or necessity alone. They need dimension. They desire finally an elevation in space. The poet of vision understands the auditory and emotional needs of the words and frees them so that the word becomes both an elemental and physical being, and continuous in movement.

Eventually as the poem progresses the poem will find words are lifted from its page, and this is what is called flying or the poem will be known as "winged."

Now there is no reason to signal any decade as deficient of vision. Words on a page are deficient of vision. A poem breathes in the precincts of vision.

It is not the flash of "brilliance" appropriated to use its spray of technique to quench the pathos of a deprived poem we need fear. "Courageous metaphors, singular and far-fetched epithets, inversions, placement of words, suppressions" are the suspenseful qualities Leopardi admired in Horace.

It is the counter-spirit we must be aware of. The presence of the mundane inhibits the imaginative properties of a poem, whittles its growth, cripples wing power; mundanity relegates a poem to the ash heap of words.

Green Shoots

"the grass is growing" . . . . . . allow the green shoots to be exhibited.

Young thoughts need to grow, as if they were showing in a mirror the words slowly return
to the surface, goldfish in a bowl.

the anonymous, the nameless that remains in your thoughts, don't bother to give them capital letters, be fearless in representing your thoughts, they are new today.

Be slow at first in permitting your passionate beliefs to surface; they will be pummeled on the surface of someone else's thought.

The Voice of the Poem

> the lyric, the lyre, is the voice of the poem.
> Perhaps it is a mistake to use a Greek-based word
> for the throat-box of a poem. If there is a
> desire to abolish lyricism it might be necessary
> to substitute for that word "voice" of the poem;
> you cannot abolish that. It is the activity of the
> voice on which the poem depends.

The spirit of the poem, the vision within it—if these are abolished we have a shadowy poem that only repeats the values of what is observed.

"The cat went up the wall." Then if we were to add "and the wall came tumbling down" there would be an apocalyptic inference—a sense of doom would then enter. However, in order to speak in one single note, avoiding the concept of lyricism, inside of which is vision or spirit, we might write:

That cat climbed up a wall/cats are good at climbing.
That would be didacticism and many poets rely on didacticism because they believe it is pragmatic and thus has philosophical overtones.

But where is the adventurous attitude that is the life's necessity of a poem?

We are offered a line in one enclosed space: the cat climbing a wall. How boring.

(1) Lyricism can rescue from mundanity. The worldliness of poetry.

(2) Poetry makes monstrous demands on the poet. The poem, itself, is a battlefield. But what a battlefield! And on this terrain the poet can select several weapons. One of which is nature or the green point, the green eye of vision. This greenery becomes eloquent. Nature is a quick entry into lyricism, because for one thing it is so eloquent. The poem notes the entrance of greenery, a green vision with a voice.

> Wordsworth may have overdone this as he crowded his moral view of man with nature, but what survives from his huge canvas entangled in morality and relying on nature to relieve the poem of its moralism is a lyric voice, a voice we cannot help listening to; this voice, enhanced and made eloquent by its sound, is the sound of lyricism.

Importance of *Texture* — the texture of a poem
> What does it feel like — how layered is the poem, what substance is it composed of, what does it taste like — and we learn this through the poet's manipulation of language and the control of the structure of the poem.

Allow Yourself

Allow yourself to find the archaic in a poem, like driving on rockbound surfaces. The poem needs the archaic to support it

a piece of the past /.

Bandusia

There was a blend
More than language
Tossed onto the landscape.
I looked into its pockets,
The way a library
Constructed in the Roman
Manner will increase your desire
For a vivid life,
Beyond harbor and freeways.

An acreage of water,
A mirror,
The Fountain of Bandusia
Crimsoned by the goat
Sacrificed to its splendor.
There in August the ox
Lays down his burden
To lap the sweet chill.

Endears itself to the poet
Who surveys holdings
Nourished by this fountain:
Ilex scraping the cavern,
Splashed odes
    Filling jars.

From The Odes of Horace, *Book III, Ode XII; translated by Barbara Guest.*
Originally appeared in Washington Square *magazine, January 2001.*

Early Days of a Poet

To be a poet requires that one also be a reader.

We all have shared that husky moment when, apple in hand, writing pen prepared, we knelt in obeisance to the goddess of literature. It cannot begin too early, this moment with the heart wildly beating the story. There is a story gripping the pen, and the child is often eating something sweet, the child emboldened by fruit or chocolate to write out a "funny" or "sad" story. I began my career writing about a young girl in a boarding school.

Never having set eyes on a "boarding school" I was determined to begin my story there. All sorts of difficult adventures lay in my way. It was really a *Pilgrim's Progress* I was outlining, but I had no idea of this. I had never read that book. Etc., etc. I believe there was a little whimsy in the story— some sadness, and some jokes filled the contents of a book destined never to be opened again. It was carried by mistake into the outdoors where the trashman finished the story by lighting it with a match. But I began to read. Instead of a "writer," I became a Reader.

Splendor Falls

"The splendor falls

on castle walls, and
snowy summits old in storey.

The long light shakes across the lake

and the wild cataract leaps in glory."

This introduction to a poem by Tennyson in which he invokes an introduction to high romance, battlements and song in the tradition of Victorian megalomania is one which sets the scene for a child of seven or so to
invoke all the glory of fable. It is heady romance, and it used to be that it
seldom failed. When I was young, I am convinced, this poem set me on
the road of high romance leading to a career of being a poet.

Kant Sees

Kant sees a close similarity between the artist and the dreamer, like fairies in an Irish dream; but these are involuntary dreams, outside the dream of the real artist.

The discussion of the imagination in the *Critique* continues when the *Critique* refers to the imagination as a "productive faculty of cognition." We feel that it (imagination) works in freedom from the law of association. "The productive power of the imagination is animated by spirit and this spirit is no other than the faculty of producing aesthetic ideas."

The Desire for Sensationalism in Literary Culture

How exciting to sit down.

Sensationalism! How exciting to stir the grains into a bowl of dusty poetry! To light a fire under it: to borrow new chairs to sit by its side!

To calm its sensa
tionalistic nerves! To read the Philosopher Kant! here is a gram of mustard. Here is the muscular salt. Here is a silver spoon with a coat of arms, as in the Revolution! To live during a poetic
Revolution.

       LET US OPEN THE SENSATIONAL POETIC JOURNAL. LET US TRY TO BE MORE POETIC AND HAVE OUR PICTURE TAKEN WHILE WRITING LIKE RILKE, and others.

Wounded Joy

The most important act of a poem is to reach further than the page so that we are aware of another aspect of the art. This will introduce us to its spiritual essence. This essence has no limits. What we are setting out to do is to *delimit* the work of art, so that it appears to have *no beginning and no end, so that it overruns the boundaries of the poem on the page.* All of the arts share this need for delimiting.

Coleridge said that a poem must be both *obscure and clear.* This is what we search for in our poem, this beautiful balance between *the hidden and the open.*

What is this poem that appears to be opening within our hands? Mallarmé says that "Poetry is nothing but the intensely musical and emotional state of the Soul."

Do you ever notice as you write that no matter what there is on the written page something appears to be in *back of everything that is said, a little ghost?* I judge that this ghost is there to remind us there is always more, an elsewhere, a hiddenness, a secondary form of speech, an eye blink. Not on the print before us. And yet the secret is that this secondary form of writing is what backs up the primary one, it is the *obscure essence that lies within the poem that is not necessary to put into language, but that the poem must hint at, must say "this is not all I can tell you. There is something more I do not say." Leave this little echo to haunt the poem, do not give it form, but let it assume its own ghost-like shape.* It has the shape of your own soul as you write.

John Donne wrote this very modern paragraph describing the state of his mind troubling his prayers, but he might as well be describing, and probably is, the state of his mind as he approaches a poem:

> A memory of yesterday's pleasures, a fear of tomorrow's dangers, a straw under my knee, a noise in mine ear, a light in mine eye, and anything a nothing, a fancy a chimera in my braine troubles me . . .

He can also be saying that these things trouble him as he reaches for his pen to make a poem. The presence of a hidden anxiety about a poem might be a necessary prodding to go intensely into the poem. A poem should tremble a little. Again remember, "Poetry is nothing but the intensely musical and emotional state of the Soul."

Baudelaire tells us that a poem should have within it "a dose of the bizarre." This can be a wake-up call within the poem, to say the poet is nodding, has become too mundane, too involved with a daily recounting. I love this phrase. I suppose it is the basis of Surrealism, but in Surrealism *everything is bizarre.* I prefer this little dosage. When one is nodding or recapitulating events of daily life and we become mundane, then this little *"dose of the bizarre," like holding a minnow in your hands, or a feather of a riotous color, not too much, or the bizarre will overwhelm the poem and to have nothing but a bizarre account can be very boring.*

To sail off on a ship of delight, a brief, necessary voyage within the poem to encourage pleasure, to escape the mundane, the chain of struggle. If and when necessary, this pleasure will sparkle at the hour of a poem's struggle to endure, the poem's midnight.

Remy de Gourmont suggested that the past must constantly be re-invented. As you take issue with the poetry of the past, remember that it has its usages, its declarations and affirmation, because it has existed so long. Think of the past as the modern poem runs along beside you. As the past darkens the window.

In the youth of my poetry I was fortunate to be surrounded by painters in the art movement of Abstract-Expressionism and I learned from them.

First I noticed these painters appeared to have a lot more joy than did the poets. They were more playful! Their ideas were exploding on the canvas and they had a sense of freedom the poets were only beginning to learn from them. This was perhaps a heritage of Surrealism, but the fact that they were a MOVEMENT and were accepted even by the commercial world, which meant money, lent them this freedom. The entire city of New York liked their art. More importantly the air around them was hesitating as it turned into *the moment*. The idea of a moment with its special apparatus is a good thing for poetry also.

No subject is introduced; the painting is spontaneous. The subject is found as you explore the canvas. And that is a useful idea. I remember when a painter visited and I had a little poem in the typewriter and he looked at it, the little unwritten poem, but with its title already secured. The painter said "never give a poem a title, let the poem find its subject."

Remember Picasso said, "You may give a painting a title, but it always turns out to be something else." Frank O'Hara's poem "Sardines" plays with this idea. Another thing these painters borrowed from Surrealism was the use of "accident." I know that I have accidentally typed a wrong word and thought, "well that's a better word, anyway."

Behind these sentences is the idea of no pre-planning. I can always tell when I am reading a pre-planned poem; there is no freshness in it. No mysterious element of change, as when the poem lies quivering on its page, its contents wounded, yet the poet is joyful.

An admonishment not to be fearful of tarnishing your wings. To rest in the glow of great poets; they always have something to tell you. To welcome the substance that glitters and rubs off.

I cannot end a discussion of poetics without stressing the power of the Imagination. To lean on it! To trust it! Imagination is the single most important element in poetry. When I examine a poem, it is not for its form or style. There are plenty of "successful" poems. One must look for the vibrating imagination hid under those stones of form or style. How empty is all their dazzle without imagination.

Coleridge wrote that in his youth he was *"trembling with imaginative power."* *Imagination is the absent flower of Mallarmé, a turbulent presence to be evoked.*

———

Appeared in The American Poetry Review, *September/October 2002;* *Arthur Vogelsang, editor.*

Forces of Imagination

The forces of the imagination from which strength is drawn have a disruptive and capricious power. If the imagination is indulged too freely, it may run wild and destroy or be destructive to the artist. "The frenzied addiction to art," wrote Baudelaire, is a canker that devours.

If not used imagination may shrivel up. Even in old age Goethe wrote that he feared the wild tricks of a lively imagination. "What is the good," he said, "of shaping the intellect, securing the supremacy of reason? Imagination lies in wait."

Plato also suspected imagination. He thought man could be transformed by the imagination and suggested laws that would prohibit the miming of extravagant evil characters. He advised changing from the dramatic to narrative language if writing became overwrought. It is fear of what begins as fiction ending as reality.

Plato said, "If any poet were to come to us and show his art we should kneel down before him as a rare and holy and delightful being, but we should not permit him to stay. We should anoint him with myrrh and set a garland of wool upon his head and send him away to another city."

These words express fear of the possibility of a destructive risk that lurks in poetry. Baudelaire continually reminds us that the magic of art is inseparable from its risks. And this risk is also a necessary component of poetry as it performs its balancing act between reality and the imaginative force at work within the poem. The poet enters the poem with a hood over the poet's eyes. The poet has arrived from a distance from a real world. The poet is conjurer balancing on the barre of risk like a dancer, or acrobat. Have you ever wondered why the painter is prone to painting acrobats, and not only in the famous painting of Picasso. It is because in all the arts, the practitioner—the poet, the artist, even the musician—with a new set of rules, maintains a balancing act between reality or rules, and the imagination. And there is where the risk lies, in that balancing act, so filled with fervor and terror as the little word is placed on its spool of light.

Hegel's language is radical. He believes that art exists in absolute freedom and is allowed to attach itself freely, he says, to any form it chooses that will help it "exercise the imagination." We can view the poem as existing for a time in pure space, exercising imagination, no matter how mundane the exercise may appear, how untidy the bag of words it carries with it. The poem is enjoying a spatial freedom before it settles into images and rhythm and order of its new habitat on the page.

In this state of suspension the art that is created is infinitely susceptible to new shapes because no shape can be regarded as final. No form is safe when the poet is in a state of perpetual self-transformation, or where, as Hegel suggests, the artist is in a condition of "infinite plasticity." This position of "subjectivity" or "openness" the poem desires to obtain, free to be molded by forces that shall condition the imagination of the poet.

In the sixteenth century Ariosto complains that chivalry is being destroyed by the introduction of firearms. This is what *Orlando Furioso* is about, and I borrowed the title in my own mock epic, *Rocks on a Platter*. In *Orlando Furioso* we are given a setting of pure fantasy, and fantasy is written all over the poem. The reader can have no doubt of its unreality.

It is the innovation of Ariosto we admire, an alarming innovation that bespeaks the power of innovation when we are told the poem may have aided in the destruction of the codes of chivalry.

The idea of "infinite plasticity" is a noble one. It causes the poet to breathe more freely. One thinks of *Prometheus Unbound*. And it is the blood of "boundlessness" that enters the poem.

When I was a young poet I was immensely influenced, as you know, by painters with whom I circulated. Their ideas of painting took up my young life. I envied their freedom. I began to use some of their methods. Often titles arrived after the poem was finished, as O'Hara's illustrates so humorously in his poem "Sardines."

The idea belonged to Picasso, who said about subject matter: "You have to have an idea of what you are going to do, but it should be a vague idea. It's always something else in the end." This idea of Picasso's also, for some reason, lends an idea of space to the poem.

Painters also gave me a sense of being unconfined to a page. I became experimental without using that word. I wrote *"Parachutes, My Love, Could Carry Us Higher"* without considering whether my parachutes went up or down.

The Hollywood songwriter Johnny Burke wrote, "Imagination is funny, it makes a cloudy day sunny."

André Breton said, "to imagine is to see."

―――――

A talk given at her award ceremony for the Robert Frost Medal for Lifetime Achievement in Poetry, at the Poetry Society of America, April, 1999. Published in The American Poetry Review, *September/October 2002; Arthur Vogelsang, editor.*

Artist Laurie Reid collaborated with Barbara Guest on a previous book, *Symbiosis* (Kelsey St. Press, 2000). Reid's work has been exhibited at the San Francisco Museum of Modern Art, the 2000 Whitney Biennial, and The Drawing Center, New York. Images included here are:

(COVER)   *X-1,* 2000, color spit bite aquatint, 5 × 40″
(PAGE 24)   *Kathryn's Piece,* 1997, watercolor on paper, 33 × 30″
(PAGE 35)   *Elements (C),* 2000, spit bite aquatint, 10 × 9″
(PAGE 60)   *Elements (A),* 2000, spit bite aquatint, 10 × 9″
(PAGE 86)   *X-1,* 2000, color spit bite aquatint, 5 × 40″
(PAGE 97)   *Antidote,* 2000, watercolor on paper, 80 × 12″

All images appear courtesy of the artist,
Stephen Wirtz Gallery and Crown Point Press.

─────────

The text of *Forces of Imagination* is typeset in Berkeley, originally designed by Frederic Goudy in 1938 for the University of California Press in Berkeley. (This 1983 version is a redrawing by Tony Stan.)

The display font is Frutiger, designed by Adrian Frutiger in 1968 for signage compatible with the architecture of the Charles de Gaulle Airport outside Paris (with additional weights added in 1976).

Book designed by Poulson/Gluck
Printed by McNaughton & Gunn